Visualization-Based Manifestation

Visualization-Based Manifestation

Table Of Contents

Foreword

Visualization refers to the practice of seeking to impact the outer world by altering one's thoughts and expectations. Visualization is the fundamental technique underlying positive thinking and is frequently utilized by athletes to enhance their performance. Visualization is the technique of utilizing one's imagination to visualize particular behaviors or events occurring in one's life. Get all the info you need here.

Manifesting With Visualization

Chapter 1:

Synopsis

Advocates propose producing a detailed schema of what one wants and then visualizing it again and again with all of the senses (i.e., what do you see? what do you feel? what do you hear? what does it smell like?). For instance, in sports a golfer might visualize the perfect stroke again and again to mentally train motor skills memory.

The Basics

In one of the most long-familiar studies on visualization in sports, Russian scientists equated four groups of Olympic athletes in terms of their physical and mental training ratios:

- Study group 1 got 100% physical training;
- Study group 2 got 75% physical training with 25% mental training;
- Study group 3 got 50% mental training with 50% physical training;

Study group 3 had the best performance outcomes, indicating that particular sorts of mental training, like consciously invoking particular subjective states, may have significant measurable impacts on biological performance.

According to experts, "The Soviets had ascertained that mental images may act as a prelude to muscular impulses.

It has since gotten to be more widely understood and accepted in neuroscience and sports psychology that subjective training may cause the body to react more favorably to consciously desired results.

Visualization practices are a typical form of spiritual exercise. In Vajrayana Buddhism, complex visualizations are utilized to attain Buddhahood, e.g. Generation Stage. Additionally, visualization is utilized extensively in sports psychology.

A few celebrities have endorsed the utilization of visualization and claimed it had a substantial role in their success. Such celebrities include Oprah, Tiger Woods, Arnold Schwarzenegger, Anthony Robbins, Bill Gates, Ronnie Bernard and other people.

In a 2008 interview with Tavis Smiley, actor Will Smith said he utilized visualization to defeat challenges and, as a matter of fact, visualized his success years before he got to be successful.

A different example is actor Jim Carrey, who wrote out a check to himself in 1987 in the sum of 10 million dollars. He dated it 'Thanksgiving 1995' and put in the notation, "for acting services rendered." He visualized it for a long time and in 1994 he got $10M for his role in Dumb and Dumber!

Chapter 2:

Synopsis

The word "manifesting" means to make something real or readily perceived by the senses particularly by sight (this is the definition in the Dictionary).

About Manifesting

The word may be applied in a lot of ways depending upon the context. For our use, manifesting may be applied as we wish to materialize our desires, goals & dreams that merely take their forms in our minds. Oh no, this won't give you the power to control other people as no one can do that. Each of us was given a free will and we ought to utilize that will to make conscious choices so that we'll achieve our highest potential.

Manifesting is a means of empowering us. It enables us to take control of our lives rather than simply leaving it to chance and fate. It presents us the power to transform our thoughts into something that is true and material to us.

If you continue thinking about cash, a picture of a one dollar bill or a check will come into your brain. One of these days this will get to be an experience for you in your reality.

You may see a one dollar bill on a billboard or hear somebody talk about cash. Naturally if you only see it or hear about it but not own it, it's of no use to you. You may as well try a different way of manifesting it.

While manifesting is a gift meant to grant our wishes, it will work against us if we don't arrive at a conscious choice of what we're going to manifest. We could manifest even if it's something we don't want as long as we hold the thought of that object or idea in our brain.

Everybody has the natural power to manifest anything they want into their life. It's simply that we were not taught this reality growing up, and we were unconsciously programmed with so much data that we have simply forgotten our innate manifesting attractive power. The truth is we're each overflowing with this energy, yet it might be "sleeping" inside you. With this ancient manifesting knowledge and an inspired action m manifesting routine...it could be awakened.

Whatever you hold your focus upon, you're manifesting THAT into your life faster than you might realize. If you're constantly focusing on what you DON'T want to think, feel, or experience then you'll see that is precisely what you're manifesting.

By learning these ancient secrets of manifesting, you are able to remain centered, peaceful and focused on what you DO want to think, feel and experience. From this place, you'll discover that your greatest dreams and desires will manifest into your world.

Manifesting is an astonishing gift that wields power to fulfill our deepest desires as well as our greatest fear, so utilize it wisely...

Chapter 3:

Deciding What To Manifest

Synopsis

The statement, "You may do anything you put your mind to," leads us to think that all you have to do is imagine what you'd like to achieve, set your mind to the task, and await success.

To a certain degree, this is true. Centered intention blended with action is a potent force. However the statement is misleading as it fails to mention the difficulty and necessity of centering your mind on a particular goal.

What Do You Want

Most of us do not know what we wish. We believe we do, however we truly do not. We only know what we do not wish. We do not wish an awful job. We do not wish to be destitute. We do not wish to disappoint our family.

Knowing specifically what you wish is much different than recognizing what you do not wish. When you solely know what you do not wish, your intentions aren't focused and you manifest the bad. Consider this illustration.

Bill doesn't wish to be destitute. He's sick of bringing in less than his friends, and he's determined to advance his status. To achieve this goal, Bill could take a lot of different paths. He could train for a high paying job, like doctor or lawyer. He might begin his own company, go into real estate, or do a lot of other things that would lead to bringing in wealth.

However Bill isn't sure what he wants to do. He doesn't understand which path best fits his skills and personality, so he doesn't resolve to follow any certain path.

Hoping to answer this question, he investigates a many possibilities, however as soon as he runs into hardship he decides that path isn't for him and moves on to a fresh solution.

Bill's actions aren't centered. Although he works really hard, his efforts do not build on one another. Instead of building one giant impenetrable sand castle, Bill has established 20 little ones that are easily toppled. He winds up confused and disheartened. Finally Bill's lack of focus leads to failure.

Now, what if Bill had selected a particular path, particular goals to manifest? Suppose he chose on the law profession. His actions and things to manifest would have been clearly defined:

- Get a elevated score on the LSAT
- Get letters of recommendation
- Become accepted at a great law school
- Choose a field of law
- Gain a law degree
- Find a high paying job with a great law firm

A set of particular goals is much simpler to accomplish and to manifest than a vague end goal like getting rich. Being centered on a path gives Bill a logical set of actions to manifest. Each achievement is one step closer to the final goal.

I think we may all agree that committing to a distinctly defined path for manifesting, regardless of which one, gives Bill the greatest chance of getting to be wealthy.

However how may he select a path if he doesn't know what he wants? Perhaps cash isn't his only goal. Perhaps he wishes to do something he loves at the same time. Perhaps he can't afford to go back to school. Realism is complicated, and Bill doesn't wish to commit too soon.

And that's why he fails.

However I do not think that's inevitably a bad thing. Most individuals do not fit neatly into a predefined path. Forcing yourself into one might lead to success; however it likely won't make you happy.

This is the point. If you wish to be conventionally successful, to attain riches and status, you have to choose a particular path (preferably something mainstream) and work at manifesting each step.

On the other hand, if you aren't especially concerned with riches or success, you may take your time searching for that perfect life.

Just do not wait too long to choose. Every moment you deliberate, is a moment you lose.

.

Chapter 4:

How Visualization Works

Synopsis

Understanding how visualization works helps in visualizing better. Using a technique mindlessly might not yield the desired results.

How It Works

The mind is made up of 2 parts, the conscious mind and the subconscious. We think with our conscious or rational mind and whatsoever we think repeatedly sinks into our subconscious mind or creative mind. The subconscious is like a computer. It can't think on its own, it can't differentiate between good and bad, between true and false. It takes on face value, whatsoever is presented to it.

When the conscious mind gives the subconscious the same thought over and over, it begins taking the thought seriously and sets out bringing it into existence.

Our life of experiences are stored in the subconscious to which it has access. It likewise has access to the Universal mind for which nothing is inconceivable.

The subconscious then brings about conditions in which our repetitive thought is manifested.

I once read a story which demonstrates how visualization works in a spectacular, though damaging, way. (So, 'be careful what you ask. You might get it.')

A guy had a daughter who had terrible arthritis. He tried a lot of medications but without result. Whenever he would meet somebody, he used to say, "I'll give my right arm to cure my daughter" naturally he made the remark figuratively however he made it again and again.

Strangely, a few years later, when he was travelling in an automobile, he met with an accident in which his right arm was torn from his body. Inside a few days, his daughter's arthritis was cured!

In order to understand how visualization works, we have to comprehend that the pre-eminent language of the subconscious is pictures.

Though it translates words equally well, it's more easily shaped by pictures. That's why visualization is so effective in making your subconscious deliver to you whatever it is that you wish.
It's likewise crucial to visualize only the ending result and not the procedure. We have to tell the subconscious only what we wish. Leave it to the subconscious to decide the procedure of getting it.

A picture is worth 1000 words. We've all heard that saying previously! This has never been truer than in the case of utilizing visualization. Visualization is a great tool to deal with the disease and sickness in your life. Visualization, a meditation method, utilizes pictures or imagery to balance the mind and boost our body back to total wellness. The brain is divided into 2 sides - our left logical side and our right creative side. Most of our life is spent utilizing the left, logical side of the brain. By utilizing visualization we yield to our right creative side and get a balance of the brain. This balance helps the natural healing procedures of the mind and body.

Visualization utilizes imagery to alter your emotions, which alters your feelings, which then turns into physical sensation that may relieve or eliminate symptoms.

The mental form of the mind is emotion and emotion brings about feelings. The body s physical form is sensation. When we get an emotion it brings about a feeling that turns into a physical sensation. Visualization supplies positive images for the brain that change your emotions that produce a feeling which turns into a sensation.
That s how you get at your mind-body connection.

Most times we're in logical, left brain mode for survival. This induces an imbalance in the brain. By giving in to our right brain we access the mind-body connection which fixes the balance of the brain and opens us up to change and replenishment.

It has been demonstrated that negative emotions lower our immune system and keeps us mired mentally. Having negative emotions delays and stops us from achieving our goals and really inhibits the brain in achieving what we wish. Positive emotions really boost the immune system and make the brain work in a balanced mode which is conducive to change.

The process to visualization is easy. 1) Find a calm place. 2) Define your intent. 3) Center on the breath and breathing. 4) Start your visualization. Visualization commonly takes a few weeks to work and ought to be done in the morning and at night before bedtime. But, many individuals find results after the very first time. To have a successful outcome, you have to be specific when you define your intent and feel, realize and believe that it is going to work!

Chapter 5:

Getting In The Right Mindset

Synopsis

Another step in the creative visualization procedure is to learn how to trust that you already have your specified outcome in the here and now. This isn't about wishful thinking or betraying yourself. It is about recognizing the truth behind reality creation and having the sort of faith that's the "evidence of things not seen".

Your Mindset

What is included in believing: To believe something is to sincerely know it. It is to no longer have to think about it. If you trust you have your intent in your here and now you do not have to be in a place of anticipation or wondering where it is as you already have it. During your visualization sessions, trust that you already have what you intend by seeing yourself amply experiencing the choice itself. The words of Jesus perfectly capture the essence of how to believe: "What things so ever you ask for when you pray, believe that you receive them, and you shall have them" (Mark 11:24).

So how to get in the right mindset and believe: Relax utilizing the relaxation techniques below.

Find yourself a quiet place where you know you won't be disturbed for at least one-half hour. Sit straight in a comfy seat with your feet on the floor, your back supported and your hands resting on in lap. You may choose to lie down if you prefer as long as you are able to keep yourself from falling asleep during the procedure.

Close your eyes and take 3 to 5 deep, abdominal breaths. Breathe in deeply and steadily through your nose letting your stomach rise slightly or push out. This loosens up your diaphragm and helps more air to enter your lungs. Hold your breath momentarily and then breathe out slowly through your mouth, letting your stomach return to its normal position.

To make certain you're using right breathing techniques, place your hand on your tummy and practice this breathing technique. This is the right way to breathe. Train yourself to effortlessly breathe this way correct through your visualization sessions.

Mentally count down slowly from twenty-five to one while you continue to breathe deeply. If you discover that counting backwards doesn't bring you to a relaxed state, try beginning from fifty or as high as needed. In the same way, with practice you might discover that counting back from as little as ten is adequate to accomplish the same state of relaxation.

Next, bring to your mind something which you already possess with out-and-out certainty, be it the roof over your head, your sight, your automobile or even just knowing where your next revenue is going to come from. Note how your body and mind react to having something with such certainty. You're likely to feel no tension, no strain, no worry, no wondering where it is, no desiring - just the serenity and stillness that comes with knowing. Allow yourself to amply experience this state of knowing what it means to have something. Repeat this exercise on a regular basis and soon you'll have learnt how to believe and will be able to re-create and transfer the feeling of trust to those things you intend to experience during your visualization sessions.

Chapter 6:

Synopsis

All of us are really busy producing our personal reality. Creativity is a full-time job and we're all rather good at it. Problem is, most of the time we do this unconsciously. That means that there's a strong possibility we utilize our energy to manifest things we don't truly want.

What We Focus On

Because creative thinking is part of our nature we're commonly not consciously aware of our role in the creative process. There's a natural tendency to resist the idea that we're the ones producing it. This is peculiarly true when we manifest a reality that we don't truly love.

Till we're ready to acknowledge the role our personal creativity plays in our own reality we'll likely carry on to manifest results we would rather keep away from.

We've talked numerous times about utilizing the power of focus to help us achieve our goals. But without direction, focus may in reality cause us to manifest the very things we're trying to keep away from. As a matter of fact, an avoidance mindset may program us to use our creativity to continually produce the precise things we don't need.

Here's what happens if we try to avoid something. Let's suppose it's a frigid winter day and there's ice on the walk. Obviously, you don't wish to slip on the ice and fall. So, as you go out the door you think to yourself: "Be cautious, don't slip on the ice."

Your brain can't process the thought "don't slip on the ice" without seeing you slipping on the ice. What have you just accomplished? You've just utilized your creativity to form a mental picture of yourself slipping on the ice, and now that's what you're focused on. The slicker the walk, the more you'll focus on that mental picture.

Can you see where this is leading? You're walking down a tricky path and your brain is centered on an image of you slipping and falling. The harder you focus, the more likely you are to slip and fall down. In this case, you' are using the power of focus to manifest the very situation you are trying to avoid.

One of the things that reveal what we're focused on is our speech. Do you tend to discuss issues, or opportunities? Do you contribute to damaging conversations, or do you endeavor to shift the conversation in a more favorable direction?

Is your conversation encouraging, or discouraging? Do you discuss what's wrong with your life, or do you share the things you're thankful for? Do you have a complaining spirit, or do you look for the favorable aspect of any situation?

Most of us like to think of ourselves as having a favorable outlook. If that's true, then it will be seen in our conversations. So I encourage you to take a close look at your pet topics for discussion, and see if there's any room for modification. We tend to talk about the things that we're centered on.

Chapter 7:

Synopsis

Have you attempted to manifest lots of positivity in your life only to discover yourself disappointed, frustrated or uninspired by the results? If you've said sure...

You're NOT alone! The bare truth is that most individuals will never get the sorts of transcendent and life altering experiences they want from Law of Attraction kinds of exercises, and that's an unfortunate and really sad fact.

The simple truth is that visualization works! It works well, it works quickly...and it works for everybody.

Mind movies are fairly new phenomena that have swept the web in recent months, but in truth, are simply a great way of employing modern technology to dateless wisdom and truths.

The Images

How they work is really simple. Mind movies act as visual representation of your perfect life. Your greatest self. Your peak self, and in the places that matter most...the life that you'd truly love to be living.

Mind movies, as they're frequently referred to in spiritual healing and other therapies, are visual personal development tools. They comprise of personally picked out (or mass produced) positive visual images of one's perfect life, written or verbal positive affirmation about an individual and their life.

Positive thoughts that are generated by watching or listening to mind movies, will act as a big eraser which we may use to erase, then substitute damaging programming from our brains.

There are a lot of ways of creating your own mind movie. From producing the vision of your ideal life, in a big scrap book, or on a cork board, to sophisticated self-driven net software.

Like with anything in life, it's the effort that counts and the more creativity you put into it, the more effect it will have on your subconscious mind and conscious mind.

In the average individual's life, there are a lot of situations that will provide or produce damaging energetic effects: dampening the spirit, stocking up negativity, finally turning into negative or disempowering believes which will in turn produce damaging emotional reactions, which if persistent and endured long enough, may cause psycho-somatic illness.

Put differently, negative emotional states which are endured for long time periods will solidify in the body in the form of a disease, either physical or mental and cause us to not have the life we want.

From the individual who always seems to be around to let you know that you can't succeed, to challenges that appear to be unattainable regardless how hard we try, using mind movies may be a powerful tool in breaking the damaging pattern in one's life.

Create your own video utilizing online software or create your own vision book, a collage of photographs representing your goal, an ideal situation you want to find yourself in, business accomplishment, romantic dreams, anything.

With those, you'll be looking to mix and match positive affirmations, brief statements of desire which you wish to become true in the future. If you're utilizing an online software tool, you are able to choose your own song.

Watch the video you've produced, or browse your vision book, or stand in front of your vision board and engage with what you see and hear on each level.

The basis of this principle is that you center on what you wish to the exclusion of everything else, which is the most powerful force in the Universe. The old adage "Energy goes where attention flows" is 100% true.

Chapter 8:

Visualization Exercises

Synopsis

Visualization is a process utilized by winners in all walks of life. If you truly wish something to come to fruition, put your imaginative brain to work. See the result in front of you, play the game you are going to play in your brain or watch yourself getting what you want. The only limit is your own mind.

Things To Do

You can utilize visualization to develop new habits, like eating healthier or eating slowly which prevents overeating and obesity; have you ever seen an aerobatic airplane pilot visualizing his/her routine on the ground utilizing only the hands and the imagination? Have you ever practiced a job interview in your brain?

Visualize the activity, event or result wanted. Think "what you see is what you get" and be ready for creative thinking and mind synthesis to take the lead. If you wish to construct a solar powered train, visualize this train in your brain, with its solar panels, its glittering exterior, traveling at a speed that you think it would be capable of. Dream of it, work it through your mind and let it evolve in pictures.

After you have spent a minute, day, month or even a long time visualizing the possibilities, now switch to focus mode. Right at the minute before you perform the activity, job or event that will accomplish an outcome or even the outcome towards your goal, center clearly on the picture of the action you're about to make.

For instance, if you're trying to hit a ball, picture hitting it distinctly in your brain stroke by stroke, at the correct height and the correct speed. Watch the ball being hit by your instrument, flying through the air and landing wherever it's meant to land. Add all senses to the experience, hear the nearing ball, hear and feel the impact, smell the grass. Then do it for real.

Nothing is going to get better when you feel crappy about yourself and your chances in life. A favorable mindset will reset a period of bad luck. It will turn that half empty glass into the half full glass; the rainy day into the silver-lined cloud. Grab opportunities to change and march on.

Anyone who wants change overnight will be frustrated. Even if you won a fortune in the morning, you'd be as disgruntled with your life in six months time as you're now unless you look inside to what ails you. Rather, plan to make actualization of your hopes and dreams long term.

Visualize where you'll be in five, ten and twenty year's time and the types of outcomes you wish. However don't just make a shallow photo of you in a fancy car surrounded by a big house, massive diamond collection and groveling friends.

That's hokey and won't prove healthy or satisfying in the long run. Rather, visualize what you wish to accomplish as a human and what legacies you'll leave your community and world.

Visualization only works when you're calm, comfortable and willing to give yourself time to center in peace, free from worries. Visualization is a process very close to meditation, only it's more active and vivid. In visualization, you're encouraged to think actively about the possibilities but as with meditation, you have to leave aside anything extraneous to your dreams and goals and only center on them.

It's not enough to wish to be the president. You have to consider the qualities that will help in getting to this goal. Visualize not only the presidency but likewise the skills of open communication, strength, smiling, sharing, listening, talking, being able to avert criticism with skill and respect etc. It's likely there will be skills you have to work on but again, utilize visualization to centre on separate skills to bring them up to par.

Chapter 9:

Advantages And Disadvantages

Synopsis

There are a lot of benefits of visualization and on this chapter you'll discover some of those benefits and why it's important to visualize. I'm sure once you begin visualizing, you'll discover your own benefits, but for now I will discuss the advantages and disadvantages I've found.

The Good And Bad

Visualization is a form of relaxation. The simple act of calming your mind and visualizing something cuts down the amount of tension you're constantly bombarded with on a day-to-day basis. So, if you don't visualize for any other reason, I advocate you do it for this one.

Visualizing something that you wish to have or wish to experience may bring great joyfulness into your life. We may not be in the position right now to do or have what we wish, but we may visualize it.

This is the next best thing to really having it or doing it. Our minds don't understand the difference in visualization and really having or doing a thing, so it will react in the same way it would if you where really experiencing that which you're visualizing.

With visualization there are no restrictions. You can be and accomplish anything. You can live in the home of your dreams, drive the automobile you want, be married to the love of your life and travel to different places. Not all of us get this luxury right now, however when we visualize, we have the might to visualize whatever we want without limits.

If you quiet your mind to visualize, you're actually bettering your power to focus. You no longer are bonded by the restrictions of your day. The more you visualize, and the better you get at it the better your total focus gets.

You are able to gain inspiration and you will be able to become inspired to take action towards your dreams by taking the time to visualize them. We're more likely to believe in and to move forward towards or dreams, if we can actually see them as possible and visualization may do that for us.

Disadvantages of visualization are hard to find. The most common is the time it takes out of the day to do so. However taking this time can be greatly beneficial.

Chapter 10:

Conclusion

If you don't love the reality you have been producing you are able to alter it. However to do that, you first need to accept your role in the creative process. You have to take responsibility for the reality you manifest. When you do that you'll empower yourself to produce the life you truly want.

Don't get to be a victim of negative target fixation. Don't allow outside influences to poison your mind with negative propaganda. Center your creativity on where you wish to be and fully accept your role in what you manifest. Then get ready to be amazed as the doors of possibility swing open and your life takes on a totally new dimension.